Where To Go For a Seven-year Cycle

The Fishermen's Bastion in Buda's Castle district.

Lyn Drummond

Where To Go
For a Seven-year Cycle

The author thanks Sarah Pickette and Tina Perinotto
for their apt editorial advice.

Where To Go For a Seven-Year Cycle
ISBN 978 1 74027 671 9
Copyright © text Lyn Drummond 2011
Cover photo and photos between pages 40 and 41 © Lyn Drummond 2011
Other photos © Nicola Brackett 2011

First published 2011
Reprinted 2017

GINNINDERRA PRESS
PO Box 3461 Port Adelaide SA 5015
www.ginninderrapress.com.au

Contents

Introduction		7
1	Sydney 2002	9
2	The four states of Micronesia	11
3	Chuuk and the Truck Stop Hotel	13
4	Budapest, February 2003	16
5	Hungry in Hungary	19
6	Cinderella will go to the ball	22
7	Living in a former Jewish ghetto, 2005	24
8	A new career, 2006–2007	27
9	Lisbon, Madrid, Moscow, Kiev	30
10	Romania	32
11	The EU bites home businesses	34
12	Hungarian music turns a key	36
13	Sarajevo emerges into tourism	38
14	Recession stalled among wild beauty, 2008	41
15	The sworn virgins of Montenegro & Albania	46
16	Krakow, the salt mines and Auschwitz	49
17	Berlin and the Ampelmannchen	51
18	The Czech Republic	52
19	Slovakia	53
20	Croatia	55
21	Slovenia	57
19	How's your love life?	58
20	A different relationship, Budapest 2009	60
21	Sydney, January 2010	64
22	Sydney, March 2011	68

Central Budapest.

Introduction

It was only when I had completed seven years of travelling and was considering this book that I read something about being in a so-called seven-year cycle of life which is claimed to form the basis of experience in every person's life at particular ages. The Swiss psychiatrist, Carl Jung and other notables such as German philosopher, Friedrich Nietzsche, developed a theory about these cycles of life they called individuation. Jung describes individuation as the process through which people move toward self-realisation, supposedly the ultimate goal of living. Jung described it as the process of becoming aware of oneself, of one's make-up, and the way to discover one's true, inner self.

I have interpreted individuation as meaning that we sometimes need to create something different from who we have been – if our circumstances allow and we have the courage – and leave part of that newer self in the world for some serious contemplation. Simply put: make a worthwhile mark before you dive into oblivion. Which seems a rather obvious *raison d'être* for most of us beings. I assume we are meant to be constantly moving from birth until the final cycle of eighty-four years on, hoping to achieve this aim.

I relate to Frieda Fordham's view in her book *An Introduction to Jung's Psychology*,* where she says individuation is not usually an aim or an ideal for the very young, but rather for the older person or for those who have been impelled by some specific experience, sometimes traumatic, to leave the so-called safe paths and look for a new way of living.

The problem of the second half of life is to find a new meaning and purpose in living which sometimes is best found in the under-developed side of the personality which can be repressed in the pursuit of ambition. Many people cannot face this opportunity and prefer to hang on to the values of youth, she writes.

An Introduction to Jung's Psychology, Frieda Fordham, Penguin, 1966

Why seven cycles? My research gave no exact answer. Except from ancient times seven has been seen as a mystic or sacred number. Composed of four and three, these numbers were lucky to the ancient Pythagoreans – who believed in the transmigration of the soul after death into a new body, human or animal. There are seven days in the week, seven graces, seven deadly sins, and the seventh son of a seventh son was considered noble – this favoured number has much support.

I had been in the ninth seven-year generic cycle, from age fifty-six to sixty-three, where I was supposed to appreciate the wisdom wrung from my life's experiences (not sure about wisdom; more often pain and bewilderment at certain inexplicable events); to be able to give sound advice (only when asked, I add) and to not be disheartened when no one takes any notice of you, no doubt discarding you in certain predominantly Western cultures because of your age rather than your experience (my words). Moral: don't tell anyone your age, as society will judge you by that.

While we are on the seven-year thing, really a hook to hang this book's title upon, allow me to briefly dwell on that famous Shakespeare soliloquy from *As You Like It* that begins 'All the world's a stage'. It presents seven stages in the life of man. In a speech from Act II, scene 7 of the play, Jacques, one of the groups of noblemen living a life of exile in the Forest of Arden, speaks of the seven stages: infant, school boy, lover, soldier, wise man, old age, second childhood – with the end marking a return to the beginning, if you count the 'mere oblivion' of second childhood as similar to the 'muling, puking infant' of the start. If second childhood – in that final seven-year cycle – is about playing more and retaining a sense of wonder through the revelation of new experiences, as I have been attempting to do these past seven years, then bring it on.

1
Sydney 2002

Tantalising strands of anticipation pluck at my discouragement on a warm, spring evening in Sydney. The adrenalin is palpable in crowds heading out for the night, work discarded probably hours before. I have just left work. Media deadlines have been met, but there's a nagging. Self-pity? Maybe. Feeling manipulated by those who leave on time and me behind alone to pull the pieces together. I stop metres from a bus heading home. Let it go. Enough. I am leaving. Don't know where or even when or why at this point, but I am certain.

That was January. By July I had rented out my home and was living on Weno, the tiny capital of Chuuk, a remote island in the Federated States of Micronesia. When I return, it is for only four months before I leave again for Budapest, Hungary's fascinating capital, which I would forge a special relationship with, the gateway to a region – central and eastern Europe – I had not been interested enough in before to fully discover. This despite four years working in Brussels and arriving there in the astonishing year of 1989. I did see Prague not long after the Velvet Revolution and also the collapse of the Berlin Wall, but the rest of that region was a mystery.

The reasons I left Australia in 2002 are not clear-cut. I had attempted to ground myself by buying a home in Sydney in 2000, some five years after my husband's sudden death, and the loss of a career in the foreign service through redundancy six months afterwards. There had been other work and relationships but something fundamental was missing I could not define. I believe I was also simply bored with living in a country I knew so well.

I was also in the difficult situation many migrants find themselves in as they age – something that doesn't matter when they launch off excitedly to exotic climes – of having elderly parents the other side of the world, and immediate family in Australia. But this is a travel book and I don't wish to analyse the reasons for journey, simply that my yearning for new experiences and adventure has always been inherent and there was really no need to hunker down any more.

After unsuccessfully trying to get work as a volunteer abroad for longer periods, I registered with an aid organisation in Canberra which specialises in short-term assignments. Within two months I was asked if I was interested in a three-month stint on Chuuk, a speck in the north Pacific, one of the Federated States of Micronesia located north of the equator between Hawaii and the Philippines.

2
The four states of Micronesia

Eyes rolled and the jibes began when I told friends and colleagues I was going to Chuuk.

'Chook,* eh,' they chortled.

'It was once called Truk and it's a diver's paradise,' I countered indignantly.

'Oh yeah? Never heard of it.'

Divers do flock there because of its unique underwater graveyard of Japanese ships and aircraft, bombed by the US in 1944 during Operation Hurricane.

There are in fact more than 2,000 islands in Micronesia. In addition to Chuuk, Guam is the largest and most populated island, 543 square kilometres, at the southern end of the Marianas chain. The Federated States are Pohnpei (the capital), Chuuk, Yap and Kosrae. I visited Pohnpei and Chuuk but saw an example of Yap's stone money or *rai* in the capital.

The Yapese paradoxically dress traditionally – brightly coloured loincloths for men, and grass or woven hibiscus skirts for women – but use aid money from the US and Japan to invest in high tech. According to the Yap tourist centre, the stone money of Yap, though not legal tender in the international currency market, is still used as legal tender on the island. The value of these limestone, doughnut-shaped coins varies, though not according to size. Today the money is still owned but not moved, even though ownership may change. Most of the stone money is stored in a canal known as the money bank, though some still rests outside the men's thatched hut and family huts to denote wealth and status. Both men and women have their own traditional houses and

---

* Australian slang for chicken

you cannot enter without permission. Before World War I, women were often kidnapped and taken to the men's house, the *faluw*.

The capital Pohnpei harbours the ancient and mystical ruins of Nan Madol, which are not to be missed and still remain an archaeological mystery. The town is surrounded by a wealth of lush rainforests and waterfalls and has one small, rather ancient cinema which I savoured gleefully after a film drought in Chuuk.

Nan Madol was purported to be the ritual and ceremonial centre for the ruling chiefs of the Saudeleur dynasty. The islands were constructed by placing large rocks and fill atop submerged coral reefs to form raised platforms, which supported elaborate residential and ceremonial complexes. The complexes were built primarily from columnar basalt, a volcanic rock that breaks naturally to form massive rod-like blocks that make an ideal building material. Some weigh as much as fifty tonnes and are believed to date from 200 BC.

The highly stratified social system at Nan Madol is the earliest known example of such centralised political power in the western Pacific. Within the city, social hierarchy was reflected in the size of the residences built within the compounds, the largest being the homes of the chiefly elite. Excavations of these elite residences have revealed the presence of beads and other ornaments, which may have marked their owner's social status.

The people believe it is bewitched and won't say why. Certainly while I was there, the deadness of the trees surrounding these massive granite structures, and the sluggish water, suggested death and destruction. My guide drove me there chaotically, chewing on the red betel nut narcotic, sleeping while I explored and leaping up ready to run when I asked to leave. He told me airily on our death-defying return along tortuous roads that he didn't have a driving licence.

3
Chuuk and the Truck Stop Hotel

I arrived on the seven-square-kilometre administrative capital of Weno, via Cairns, North Queensland, Guam, and Pohnpei in late July 2002. It was humid, a steady twenty-eight degrees all year round, an ideal climate for me; pity about the isolation. I settled into a small but comfortable room at the Truk Stop Hotel after buying a bright yellow T-shirt emblazoned with Truk Stop Café, to go with the Hard Rock Café one bought elsewhere. Next door was the 'office' where I worked, occupied by my client, who slept there, one or two staff and me.

Resources were almost non-existent. My client had a laptop which she loaned me while she went overseas for five weeks, leaving me to work out what she actually wanted me to do. Not quite what I expected from the job description, which specified that all necessary resources would be provided for my work, including a computer, and that the client would be around.

Back in Sydney, the job had sounded intriguing. It included training Chuukese women in public relations, holding relevant workshops, producing a newsletter and initiating various gender awareness campaigns. The reality was very different. I was led to believe my employer ran a women's network but in fact it was only one woman who was campaigning to get into federal politics.

During her long absence, I set about planning a newsletter she had asked me to design, and getting to know a Chuukese women's group led by a formidable former matron of the local hospital, who I had long conversations with about her fascinating life. She had vigorously campaigned, almost alone, to ban alcohol on the island, and did succeed for a period. She returned to her nursing work after having children despite her husband's ultimatum – if you return to work, I leave. The work was more important, she said. He stayed.

My client's views about my role constantly changed until ultimately I had no idea what was required. I could have returned to Australia immediately, as the resources criteria had not been met, particularly after a vicious cyclone devastated the island a few weeks into my arrival, causing landslides which flattened many flimsy homes and killed hundreds, including some of my client's relatives. The aid agency asked me if I would consider it, but I was challenged and involved by then and wanted to stay. An imminent threat of cholera might have changed my mind but luckily the disease held off. So I set about having a life in this tiny place, where there seemed to be nothing to do socially.

The other volunteers on the island were from the American Peace Corps. All but one woman in her fifties, Kaye, on her first assignment, completed the two-year contract. All of them were based with the Chuukese people, sleeping on the floor with the families and eating what they ate – not always palatable. I was spoilt by comparison in my hotel room and regularly invited them for a meal. The highlight of our week was a Saturday evening church service where the singing was out of this world and then to the hotel for a burrito, which the Americans devoured as though they hadn't eaten for a week.

I went swimming most evenings in water iridescent with golden light from the setting sun, waves enveloping me like shot silk. Hiking into the hills, discovering old lighthouses where the Japanese had holed up, too war-wrecked to admire the amazing views. I helped set up a makeshift movie screen one night under the stars and enjoyed greatly *Spider Man 2* – more for location and our initiative than the film's content. I mixed with any random hotel guests, one night hitching a ride with two of them to a hastily erected backyard nightclub and dancing the balmy night away.

I walked and walked along streets marred with wrecked cars and untidily edged with shanty huts where dirty children with huge smiles waved. I found odd little stores off the tracks. One baked a daily delicious coconut cake, and it was there I also found a rare tin of baked beans, and some beef mince, which I excitedly made off with to cook savoury pancakes and beans on my mini stove.

I hitched rides with villagers on their canoes to other islands, paddling merrily with the rest, and helped with cyclone relief work, delivering food supplies to the stricken islanders who had pitched tents beside the rubble of their homes or where they used to stand, now buried under the landslides.

Australians Sally Makin and Stephen Graham, who were running the diving school in Chuuk, actually rediscovered some wrecks which hadn't been dived for thirty years. They were stunned by the treasures of the lagoon.

'Many people's favourite is *Fujikawa Maru*, a Japanese freighter which has fighter planes inside the hulls. You see bundles of shoes at the wrecks. Big shells. Sometimes you can swim through thousands and thousands of bullets, see hundreds of saki bottles. A diver once said to us, "No wonder they lost so many ships: they drank so much saki."'

Experienced Chuukese diver Kitachy Eram, from the outer island of Udot, has dived all his life. 'I lived in Saipan for four years, but I missed here,' he said, as he steered the boat around the island of Tonoas in calm aqua waters where it was hard to believe that cyclone Cha'taan had caused havoc not long before. 'I don't like places where money is all that matters. Here we spend money on food and grow our own, and don't ask for too much. As long as I can keep diving, I love it. I wouldn't want to do anything else.'

I returned to Australia from Chuuk, sad that I had not completed the extent of the work I had hoped for but with potent memories of friendships, a greater understanding of my own and others' fallibilities, and memories of the thrill of unexpectedly finding things which meant so little back home – like baked beans and coconut cakes.

The unpredictable when I returned was the offer of a contract as public affairs officer at the Australian Embassy, Budapest, starting in February 2003.

4
Budapest, February 2003

How could words displayed on shops be that long? Despite being in the centre of Europe, Hungarians speak a language unlike that of any of the countries surrounding them. Even as I write this, into my fifth year in Budapest, I still have only a handful of words. Probably not helped by my first teacher using some pretty old books, one of which told me in careful Hungarian how to rob a bank. It didn't get that desperate but the paucity of Hungarian wages – little better in 2009 than six years ago – could drive you to it.

Why was it so cold inside my apartment? Organised through an Australian who owned the Budapest apartment, it was a far better deal than going straight to a hotel, but the heating didn't work. In desperation I finally found a woman in the block who spoke French – something I did understand – and acquired some heaters until the thing was fixed.

It was a difficult transition period. That first weekend walking on the frozen parkland of nearby Margaret Island which juts into the Danube, I felt very miserable and homesick among the couples and families. But ever resourceful – and lucky to find *The Budapest Sun* and other English-language newspapers with events listed – I made contact with some expat groups, including the Hash House Harriers. This international group describes itself as an drinking club of members who walk and run occasionally; it has a lot of the rugby club atmosphere about it, with raunchy songs and crazy rules, and is not to everyone's taste, but it kick-started my social life and discovery of my new home. With them I went to Slovenia, Croatia, Czech Republic and Austria, and met hashers from all over Europe, a good ploy when travelling alone. Just check out the website of the hash group in the country you are visiting and you have an instant social life, as I discovered on first trips to Istanbul, Madrid and Barcelona.

I worked at the embassy for three years. As I had no Hungarian language, I worked with a Hungarian staffer finding sponsors for such events as film festivals and art exhibitions on a limited budget. I also wrote speeches for ambassadors, and liaised with the Hungarian foreign office on cooperative issues.

The embassy was small, the work was varied, sometimes mundane, mostly challenging, as it always is when Australia does not loom large on a European map, as I discovered when I was the public affairs manager on a diplomatic posting to Brussels for four years. Now I was at the other end of the scale, a locally engaged staffer with none of the perks of a diplomat.

'Get on with it' was the strong work message I detected, even if not said directly. You don't get any special treatment, you are like the rest of the locally engaged staff. Well, I wasn't actually – they spoke Hungarian. Friendly advice about any basic living and cultural issues would have been welcome. Like the time some months later when I was almost attacked on a tram for eating an ice cream. Apparently any kind of eating and drinking on public transport is not on, however well concealed it maybe. I asked the embassy about it and was told I was at fault of course; I was supposed to know these things. I got on with it anyway, most answers coming from friends I made who spoke Hungarian, and I tried hard to get to know a city I once heard aptly described as an old lady with tattoos.

And what of the people? When you consider Hungary's history, the ingrained melancholia of many of them is probably understandable. Even the national anthem pleads for relief from a long stretch of bad luck. Since Istvan was crowned King of Hungary in 1000, it has been overrun and oppressed by the Mongols and the Turks, then the Austrian Habsburgs, Germans and the Soviets. Exacerbating these woes was the loss of most of its land at the end of World War I under the terms of the Trianon Peace Treaty, including Transylvania to Romania.

Hungarians are upfront about any negative attitudes, almost proud, and I found much kindness too. I smiled at disgruntled shop assistants with little response, but on later visits it was improving.

It's the first country I know of to commemorate a national day because of a lost revolution (in 1848). But the point is, they tried, and at any sign of oppression the people take to the streets, like they did a few years ago when a former prime minister admitted to lying about the state of the economy. (So what's new for politicians to lie, some of you may well ask, but it was enough of an incitement for many Hungarians.)

They are also a very inventive race. From the ballpoint pen to Rubik's cube (Erno Rubik is constantly working at new puzzles). From holography to vitamin C. Albert von Szent-Gyorgyi Nagyrapolt won the Nobel Prize for Physiology of Medicine in 1937 for 'his discoveries in connection with the biological combustion processes, with special reference to vitamin C and the catalysis of fumaric acid'. The list of firsts goes on.

A first for me happened in Hungary but it was embarrassing rather than prestigious.

5
Hungry in Hungary

'You begged for food in the streets!' Family and friends were unsure whether to laugh or admonish.

Well, yes, I guess I did, if attracting a lot of attention by dramatically gesturing my hunger and thirst to the stunned and fascinated occupants of various homes can be called begging.

I had been for a long hike and didn't know the two restaurants in the town I was visiting closed at 8 p.m. and the pub only had drinks, and the owners of the house where I was staying had moved out for the night to give me some privacy and locked the fridge.

Despite more than a year living in Hungary, I still found the language very hard to express, and in this village no one understood me except the woman at the local tourist office, but she had gone home a long time ago.

I managed *kenyer* for bread and *sajt* for cheese (pronouced 'shite', or at least that was how I was pronouncing it) and *sonka* for ham. Oh, and *krumpli* for potato, a word I much preferred to the heavier *burgonya*, which I think meant the same, or maybe the former was mashed and the latter chips or... I digress. I didn't know steak or eggs but the thought of *bor* (wine) made me salivate. But that was pushing the hospitality a bit.

The village of Holloko is a delightful medieval World Heritage settlement which brims with daytime tourists. But the place was deserted by the time I returned from my walk through a tangled track to the castle.

The name Hollo (raven) and Ko (stone), pronounced ho lo koo, comes from a legend in which the owner of the surrounding castle hill kidnapped a beautiful woman whose nurse was a witch. This witch made a deal with the devil to free the woman, and the children of the devil, transformed into ravens, not only let her go but built the castle of Holloko on a nearby hill. Today their sinister black presence often guards the castle ruins.

During the day there is a stunning view over the surrounding, protected area which is part of the Bukk National Park. As dusk fell and I came suddenly on the looming and austere walls of the castle after pushing my way through particularly thick undergrowth, it was more threatening than picturesque. Hence a rather hasty descent to the village in search of company and food. None in sight.

Back first to the house where I was staying. A room which for some reason was extremely cold on a very hot day, but cheap with breakfast at 3,500 forints a night (about $23). Nothing there, so off I went in search of sustenance.

Finally a bemused family of three took pity on my antics at their front gate and ushered me in, cut two large slices of bread, buttered them, gave me a piece of cheese and a small cake, and laughed at me rather a lot, particularly one of the young men, who danced around me, giggling loudly. I went off into the night with my booty. Very grateful.

The next day my host's son, who spoke English, arrived at breakfast, related my antics of the previous night and said how amusing his neighbours had found me.

'Is there anything I can help you with now?' he grinned, passing me a fresh punnet of raspberries from the garden.

I shook my head, my mouth set in a smile, musing on how well the fruit would have gone the previous night with the *kenyer* and the *sajt* and cake. What was the Hungarian for cake?

Don't be deterred. Take a picnic to Holloko or eat before 8 p.m. It's a delightful place to visit. Buses from Budapest leaving at 8.30 a.m. and returning at 4 p.m. take just over two hours to get there.

Rooms are available in many of the local houses with families. Most of the village's sixty-seven protected peasant houses are open to the public, housing museums and folk crafts. The 400 residents are known as the Paloc people. They have their own special dialect, retaining their traditions and wearing richly decorated folk costumes.

Best times to go are for the festivals. The most spectacular festival is at Easter, when residents display not only the vibrant clothes but also the Easter customs and folk crafts.

The Raspberry Festival in July attracts many visitors as does the August Castle Tournament. A grape harvest procession is held in September and there are concerts in the castle and distinctive wooden church.

Oh, and the lunches at the two restaurants are substantial, I am told.

Next is another first which didn't quite work out the way I wished.

6
Cinderella will go to the ball

It was a dream: to go to a ball in Vienna. Ball season is January and February, so at the start of my second year in Europe I got organised. I bought a ball dress, a figure-hugging number, the pink top showing just enough cleavage, merging into a diaphanous black chiffon skirt. I hardly recognised myself. Nor did several others. Must dress up more.

Bought the shoes and bag, and managed to get invited with a group in Vienna to a ball at the magnificent Hofburg Palace. There was one problem: I didn't have a prince to swing me away into all those wonderful waltzes. But wasn't it enough to actually see the palace where the imperial family of the Habsburg dynasty ruled the Austro-Hungarian Empire for six centuries until the end of World War I in 1918? Where Marie Antoinette was born in 1755, one of Maria Theresa's (Archduchess of Austria and Queen of Hungary's) sixteen children and perhaps the most well known for tragic reasons. To gasp at the stunning fashion parade at the ball, watch the dancers whirl under the chandeliers, and hope to get asked to join them.

No.

The group I was going with was partnered, all but one other woman. They had no suggestions. I did have a relationship at the time, a man I had met shortly after arriving in Budapest, but he was away on business and didn't dance anyway. So I advertised for someone. I also contacted an escort agency, but thought it too expensive. My mistake. I had one answer to my ad, met the youngish man, rehearsed a couple of dances with him – he was good – and arranged to meet in Vienna at a pre-ball party.

He turned up just as we were about to leave for the palace. No apologies. At the ball, we danced maybe three times; he was too busy doing the rounds with whatever fresh, young things he found. I did get asked to dance occasionally, but wished heartily I had paid for an escort. You could choose latin, jazz, rock 'n' roll, but not too many Strauss waltzes in the many dance halls of the palace, which was disappointing, but the fashion parade was spectacular.

The sequel: a year later I was contacted by an American preparing to go to a Vienna ball – I had been on various dance websites looking for a partner. We agreed to meet. He even bought me a ball ticket. But an accident grounded me a week before. I hobbled to the ball but only managed one dance. Luckily another dancer was there who he knew from California – and this frustrated Cinderella left early.

Next time.

7
Living in a former Jewish ghetto, 2005

Although I have no personal experience through religion or relatives of Jewish suffering in World War II, I always felt a pang passing the courtyard of the huge synagogue at the end of the street in a former Jewish ghetto in Budapest where I rented an apartment for a year.

Here a weeping willow tree made of granite and steel commemorates all the Hungarian victims of the Holocaust. During World War II, Hungary was allied with Germany. Then, there were about 184,000 Jews in Budapest, along with an additional 62,000 people considered Jews under Nazi racial laws. About 15,000 Jews from Budapest were killed in Hungarian work camps before the Nazis invaded in May 1944. After the German invasion, a Jewish ghetto was formed in Budapest, and up to 20,000 Jews were forced to live in the synagogue complex. In the winter of 1944–1945, about 7,000 Jews living in the complex died of hunger and disease. Adolf Eichmann, reputed architect of the Holocaust, had an office in the synagogue behind the rose window in the women's balcony and the Germans used it as a radio tower. Built in 1859, the synagogue seats 3,000 people; it is the largest in Europe and the second largest in the world (after Temple Israel in New York). The interior is splendidly ornate and I was surprised at how similar it is to a Roman Catholic cathedral. Yet, despite its vastness, it is not overpowering. It was a fitting and unforgettable setting to the magnificent music at concerts I attended there one August during annual Jewish festival week.

The designated area for the ghetto was about six or seven city blocks, surrounded by a high fence, with only a handful of openings to the outside world. Guards prevented the smuggling of food into the ghetto and of Jews out. By the end of December 1944, some 70,000 Jews lived in the central ghetto in Budapest and many thousands in the international ghetto or protected houses. The same year, some 440,000 Jews were deported from Hungary to the death camps.

The Hungarian fascist Arrow Cross Party came to power during the German occupation, shooting many Jews and throwing them into the Danube River to save themselves the trouble of burials.

Visiting the Pest side of the Danube embankment near the Academy of Science in Budapest, I came across a poignant monument to this time of terror – *Shoes on the Danube Promenade*. Hungarian sculptor Gyula Pauer, and his friend Can Togay designed the monument in 2005 containing sixty pairs of iron shoes, forming a row of about forty metres, modelled on 1940s shoes. Victims had to take their shoes off before being shot as shoes were considered valuable belongings at the time.

Another reminder of that awful time came when I walked home down Raoul Wallenberg Street and glanced at the Swedish diplomat's sculpture above the street name. Wallenberg came to Budapest as secretary of the Swedish Foreign Ministry in July 1944 with instructions to save as many Jews as possible. He issued thousands of Swedish identity documents to Jews to protect them from Nazi deportation and is credited with ultimately saving as many as 100,000 people. He worked with the Swiss consul Charles Lutz, as well as Portuguese and Spanish legations, to create 'protected' houses and a 'protected' ghetto to house the Jews with international identity papers. Wallenberg was last seen leaving the city on 17 January 1945, right after the Soviet army liberated the city. But his whereabouts after that remain a mystery.

I lost track of time in Budapest's House of Terror, former headquarters for the secret police of both the Nazi and Communist governments, because the museum's evocation of that sinister era enveloped me so completely. Deeply unsettled by the visit, I relished the later relief of a walking tour with an effusive guide who showed our group a former communist flat and held us rapt about life before 1989. Out again in the bright sunshine – Hungary has more sunshine than most cities of this region – to Hero's square, across city park, the Chain Bridge and then over the Danube on a shining night to the UNESCO protected castle hill district of Buda. There is no castle, but most of the buildings in this quarter are listed monuments. Buda castle is a cultural centre which is home to the Budapest History Museum, National Gallery and some parts of the medieval fort.

8
A new career, 2006–2007

When my embassy contract ended in 2006, I hoped to find other work in Europe, but was hindered by my lack of fluency in other languages. Back in Australia for eleven months, determined to get a 'passport' to work with more mobility overseas, I took a part-time CELTA course at Sydney's University of Technology. CELTA, the Cambridge University certificate in English language teaching to adults, is tough; it was even harder for me because I was also working full-time and commuting three hours a day. But it guaranteed me work for nearly three years. However, I did not expect to get my baptism of fire in teaching at a large high school back in Budapest in 2007, my students mostly wayward fourteen–sixteen-year-olds.

Wages were very low; I earned about $750 a month teaching twenty classes a week and it helped that, being British-born, I had an EU passport. I was placed in the school under the Central European Teaching Program, a USA-based program which finds jobs for native-speaking English teachers in Hungarian schools. There is a fee to join the program but in return you are guaranteed placement for six months and can extend that time, and your visas, residency permits and health insurance are arranged for you. Accommodation is sometimes provided by the school, particularly if it is out of the city, or it is subsidised.

The experience of teaching high school students conversation English was a shock. I had the smallest, oldest classroom in this large high school and the classes were big, so there was little room to be very creative. The students were of differing levels, and getting them to speak English to me rather than their own language to each other was near impossible.

Some of the classes were more disciplined and I can be pretty strict. But I would start to feel a panic attack as I waited in the next room for the lesson to start, hearing them screaming at each other, throwing God knows what. Girls and boys lolled against each other, arms draped around shoulders, planning, I was sure, their next attack on me. I had to send two out for getting too affectionate. (Hungarians' display of public affection makes *amour* in Paris seem like a peck on the cheek.)

On a day I was going to throw it in, I discovered that Budapest-born Dennis Gabor had been a student at my school. He won the Nobel Prize for Physics in 1971 for his invention of holography, a system of lensless, three-dimensional photography that has many applications. Miklos Radnoti, considered one of the most important twentieth century poets in Hungary, had also attended the school. He was killed at thirty-five during World War II on a forced march to Germany.

Such illustrious scholars were also teenagers once, defying no doubt the good intentions of a frustrated teacher. I consoled myself that maybe I was teaching one or two with that potential. But my tenuous convictions regularly fell apart, particularly on a day when I walked in and saw 'motherfucker' written on the blackboard in various lurid colours, the class continuing to recite the word ad nauseam as though they had suddenly discovered it instead of hearing it countless times in American movies.

Furious, I ordered them out – taboo in that school. I told the school director what I had done. He monitored the class at my next lesson. Of course they behaved like angels in his burly presence but returned to form the next week after first drawing a big heart on the board, this time with 'Lyn' written in the middle of it. But many of them made me laugh too. One role play, teaching job interviews, I carefully asked a strapping fourteen-year-old with hair to his shoulders he kept slowly stroking why I should give him the job. Smoothing his hair again, he replied, disarmingly, 'Because I am very handsome.'

I left the school when my contract ended, refusing an extension, citing my preference to teach adults. Ahead was only a six-week contract at a summer school in England, so I went off to chase potential work in Lisbon, Madrid, Moscow, Kiev – which came to nought – and ultimately taught for another two years at language schools and companies in Montenegro and Germany as well as Hungary again. I worked at residential summer schools in Cambridge, England, often having to sleep in the same dorms as the teenage boys from various countries, spending half the nights dragging them out of the girls' dorms. Not fun if you need your sleep – and believe me, you do. But well paid.

9
Lisbon, Madrid, Moscow, Kiev

I probably need to explain why I didn't find a teaching job in such diverse cities. In fact, I did, but in Madrid and Lisbon offers were freelance or part-time, and I was looking for a firm contract with some security and decent money. In Madrid, sharing an apartment was the go as the wages didn't stretch to one on my own, which I preferred.

I was offered work teaching business English in Moscow, with a contract and reasonable pay, it seemed. I went and checked out the city and the workplace. Apart from the daunting idea of travelling to different companies in freezing temperatures early in the mornings and desperately trying to master Cyrillic on the complex metro system, I did not like Moscow – big, grey, generally inhospitable and extremely expensive. The school staff, run by British managers, were friendly and helpful enough, and I met two Russian friends of friends who showed me around, telling me how they had to live an hour or more out with family as they couldn't afford the city on their wages. One earned about US$1,000 a month at the US embassy.

The small bed and breakfast guest house I stayed in was comfortable and a cheap price for Moscow. The kitchen was stocked well for self-serve breakfast. There was some coming and going of young men for some reason. Vainly trying to get hold of the manager one morning to settle up, I knocked on his bedroom door several times. Suddenly the door swung open and a partially clothed young man darted into the passageway. The manager emerged sleepily to take my money.

The place was very well located, near Main Street, with its high fashion shops, similar to New York's Fifth Avenue, and a twenty-five-minute walk to Red Square. I was overwhelmed by Red Square, the Kremlin and St Basil's Cathedral and kept going day and night. Not too happy, though, about being herded out unceremoniously with others by several large men while attempting to join a church service which was half empty anyway. More about throwing weight about than no room, it seemed.

This officiousness was not so marked in St Petersburg, which I later visited (the less said the better, though, having had my purse stolen and succumbed to food poisoning there), and Kiev, capital of Ukraine.

I liked Kiev and would have taken a job there if offered. I saw St Sophia Cathedral, the UNESCO World Heritage site, and trekked around cobbled streets nearby, coming to a thankful rest at the ubiquitous Irish pub for a hearty steak. Returning to my apartment I was deafened by the instantly recognisable tones of Elton John. Loudspeakers everywhere and an excited crowd – me too – cramming around the singer on stage in Independence Square. Their chant of Elton was very different from that other chant of the Orange revolution three years before. '*Razom nas bahato! Nas ne podolaty!* (Together, we are many! We cannot be defeated!)' The mass demonstrations of that time, people sleeping in the freezing cold in makeshift tents and the euphoria of finally succeeding in getting what they wanted – the electoral triumph of opposition leader Viktor Yushchenko and victory over their country's corrupt leadership – has sadly dissipated in the inconsistent world of politics and personalities.

2007 also marked my first visit to Romania since it joined the EU in January of that year, and to Sarajevo.

10
Romania

I had been curious about Romania since 1987 when I was attached as media liaison officer to the visit to Australia of the then Romanian president Nicolae Ceausescu and his wife Elena. I was employed by the Australian Government's information service in Canberra as a public affairs officer. As part of the Australian delegation with the Department of Prime Minister and Cabinet, I was responsible for looking after the interests of both the Romanian media party and the Australian media. We flew to various Australian destinations in the president's Tarom jet allocated for the visit, savouring paper cups of water and an occasional cream cake, the only sustenance on the long stretches.

I find it extraordinary now to recall sitting behind them both – Elena was feared by all her staff from the secret police down, probably too her husband – and then in December 1989 watching them being executed after their country's revolution.

The visit passed without any public incidents, but behind the scenes it was fraught. The Ceausescus' advance party cancelled booked rooms, brought in their own chefs and food, and often ignored basic diplomatic niceties. I had my hands full keeping a rein on the Romanian media, who wanted to dash off to do interviews ad hoc and would not listen to 'a woman'.

Not too long after their return to Romania, a violent demonstration of some 30,000 workers in Brasov signalled the emergence of a solid opposition to the regime, but the full extent of the Romanian atrocities were not apparent during their Australian visit, so the Australian media was relatively easy to deal with, although I sometimes wondered if a deal was done – bad publicity equals embarrassing diplomatic incidents.

Many ethnic Hungarians in Romania live in Transylvania. Under the terms of the Trianon Treaty at the end of World War I, Hungary was partitioned, losing former territories such as Transylvania to Romania. More than one million Hungarians in Transylvania became a minority group in Romania and thousands fled to Hungary. But ethnic Romanians in Transylvania were elated at being set free from being part of the Kingdom of Hungary.

For those who stayed behind, conditions worsened under Ceausescu's regime, with its emphasis on nationalism and blatant discrimination against minorities. The Romanian history of Transylvania was highlighted in education, consistently omitting the role of Hungarians, and the Hungarian language and culture were banned. In the Transylvania villages I visited, Hungarian-speaking people recalled that time of hardship and oppression, but also how determined they were to continue on with their traditional lives and preserve their culture in unique ways in the aftermath of 1989.

June 2007 marked my second visit to Romania. The first in 2005 was a quick four-day drive heading for Bran and the so-called Dracula's Castle. Bram Stoker based his famous book *Dracula* on a nasty fifteenth century Romanian ruler called Vlad, known as the Impaler for his favourite way of killing his enemies. Legend has it that he was the vampire Count Dracula because he signed with his father's name, Dracul – Romanian for 'devil' or 'dragon'. The mystery of a vampire in Transylvania is still unsolved. But the gloomy atmosphere of the castle with its secret chambers certainly evokes the phenomena.

11
The EU bites home businesses

Five months after accession in 2007, the EU's sharp, regulatory teeth were already biting the future livelihoods of Romanian home brewers of the plum brandy known as *palinka* in Romania and Hungary, as I discovered. The potent drink is a contentious issue, with both countries claiming it as their own. Trademarks exclusive for Romania will set apart the products made in Romania from similar trademarks elsewhere in the EU, while farmers earning a living from sheep cheese production had until mid to late 2009 to meet strict new EU food safety standards.

The *palinka* brewery in the Transylvania village of Szek, which I visited with a small group on a cultural tour of the region run by Australian Sally Corrie, was closed, pending the outcome of EU quality approval of more than 400 alcohol, dairy and other food products drawn up by the Romanian Ministry of Agriculture, Forestry and Rural. But they fought back. A year later, the lower chamber of the Romanian Parliament defied a European Commission ruling and unanimously voted to eliminate excise duty on traditional home-brewed hard drinks, despite the fact that it is required to collect excise on home-brewed alcohol under the terms of its EU accession treaty.

Other traditions such as Transylvanian village music could be gone in five years according to Sally, a skilled musician, who played with the village band entertaining us as we sat, replete with local wine and food, one warm, autumn evening in the herb-scented garden of our host's home in another village, Palatka. As Szek is more isolated, in the hills on a dead end road, it still retains its musical traditions more than most Hungarian villages, despite the encroachment of Western ideas and culture. It's not just the older generation determined to keep them going – evidenced by the children singing and dancing to the band with our tour group. But lack of expertise and interest could threaten Szek's exquisite craft work. For example, Zsuzsanna Sipos is the only person in Szek prepared to make the hundreds of tiny pleats ironed into every traditional skirt so essential to the local costume.

Sara Csorba is also the sole person in this picturesque village of contrasts – no running water or bathroom at the end of one street, mod cons at the other end – to paint the delicate rose patterns in the village colours of red and blue, with a hint of yellow and green on to cabinets similar to those displayed in Szek's oldest thatched house built in 1241.

In the past, Szek's three streets – Felszeg (High Street), Csipkeszeg (Lace Street) and Forroszeg (Warm Street) – divided the town culturally as well as geographically, each street having its own dance hall (*tanchaz*), band, and regular cultural gatherings (*fono*).

This meant that children only associated with other children from their street, attended celebrations, dances and weddings there and also married others from their street. These rules relaxed in the 1980s, and the village is now more integrated – Zszusanna Sipos's sister Rozsa married a man from the third street – but it is still expected that Szeki youth will not marry out of the village. Women like Rozsa, Zsuzsanna and their mother, also Zsuzsanna, have traditionally stayed at home and work in the house and fields. They also spin, dye, weave and sew clothes, linen and blankets, and sell their handicraft at events in Romania and often in Budapest.

The last day of the five-day tour, Zsuszanna senior prepared the dish reserved for all special occasions of stuffed cabbage, a pork mince flavoured with sweet paprika, tomato, onion, garlic, pepper and smoked pork, wrapped in either pickled or fresh cabbage leaves and cooked in an open oven set in her large garden – shared with delicious home-baked bread.

Other meals we feasted on – to the accompaniment of the band – were lettuce soup made with two to three eggs, lemon juice, crushed garlic and bacon pieces, polenta with sheep's cheese – the cheese a creamy, slightly bitter taste — and delicious pastries filled with plum jam called *kifles*, which we couldn't get enough of.

12
Hungarian music turns a key

Sally, a fireball personality, has been running the tours since 2003. They were triggered by her great interest in the Transylvanian village music. She started playing the violin when she was six, growing up in the Lake George area near Canberra, but gave it up after it failed to inspire her.

When she heard her first Hungarian village music concert in London, the key turned on a new musical life that motivated her in a way her previous experience had never done. She sought out others interested in the music and together formed the band The Transylvaniacs in Sydney and joined the dance group Kengugro as a musician. She also spent ten years travelling to villages in Slovakia, Hungary and Romania researching and collecting Hungarian, Romanian and Roma village music before launching her company, Carpathian Tours.

Sally, the band and dancers have brought Hungarian and Slovakian bands and individual musicians to Australia since 1998 to take part in festivals, including the Hungarian band Tukros, which visited twice.

Sally, who speaks fluent Hungarian – having learned by listening with no formal lessons – told me between my breathless dance breaks she is passionate about the music and started the tours because she believed that the music, dance and culture was so special it should be seen and experienced by as many people as possible. The tours also provide work for the local musicians and encourage the next generation to take up the tradition.

The typical line-up for a band in Szek is, one violin, one viola and a small double bass. The viola, of a kind only found in Transylvania, has three strings instead of the normal four and a flat bridge, meaning that all three strings are played at once providing a chordal accompaniment to the violin. The bass also has only three gut strings and is played with a heavy hand made bow providing a solid, grungy rhythm and beat that can be heard without amplification by dancers at the back of the hall. Flute is played traditionally by the shepherds, but was usually given up after marriage, as it was considered an instrument for boys. The ancient melodies are influenced by Turkish, Romanian, Roma Saxon and primarily Hungarian musical history. The accompaniment is strong and simple, the bass providing the beat and the viola the off-beat. The band sits slightly behind the violin, providing a solid, strong base for the violin to improvise around rhythmically. This allows a kind of freedom within the music.

The chord structure is also simple. There are not many chords within a melody and they traditionally only play major chords regardless of the modality of the melody. The music all over Transylvania uses an untempered scale – not based on the piano tuning that we have grown accustomed to in the West. This may result in the music sounding out of tune to the Western ear, but it is in tune within its own scale, according to Sally. But, unlike others in my group, I could not adjust to the discordant notes.

Singing is a very important part of the musical culture. Children learned songs from their mothers around the house and then from their friends at the *fono*. Girls from the age of fifteen until marriage organised the *fono*, meeting early in the evening to spin, embroider, sing and dance. When the boys arrived later, they would play games, dance and sing. The gathering was still running in Szek until the late 1990s, when the pub and disco became more tantalising.

The dances at the *tanchaz* were always arranged by the boys at weekends. Traditionally, as the boys were paying for the dance, the girls had to be escorted and dance with whoever asked them. If a girl refused a dance with one of the boys, the band would stop and play the marching tune; the girl would then be escorted home and banned from the *tanchaz* for three weeks.

13

Sarajevo emerges into tourism

Edis Kolar stands at the entrance of what is left of a secret tunnel which led from his family's house in Sarajevo to the UN-controlled airport during the Bosnia–Herzegovina war. 'We have kept the transport carts, the tools for digging, the bags in which people carried food and turned it into a museum,' he said.

The museum is one of the attractions that have brought me to this once besieged city. The airport was located between Sarajevo and free territory. Any Bosnians who risked crossing it had to run the gauntlet of snipers under darkness to take food to their families, often being stopped or killed.

After the Kolar family gave their home to the Bosnian army, digging began on the secret tunnel in January 1993. Despite shelling of the work areas, it was completed and food, oil, ammunition, weapons, the injured, even goats wanting milk, were transported. Guiding me through the narrow entrance, Edis says about 300 000 citizens survived thanks to the tunnel. His grandmother, Sida Kolar, a small woman who radiated energy but preferred to leave our interview to her grandson, shunning an interpreter, was renowned for helping exhausted soldiers and giving food and winter heat in her little room to people waiting to go into the tunnel. Edis, who was eighteen at the time, and his father Bajro, who run the museum, both served in the military forces, Edis with the police and his father with the army.

While Bosnia–Herzegovina has not entirely recovered from the war, the reconstruction of Sarajevo – from its new shops and offices to the Olympic Stadium where Torvill and Dean won gold in 1984 – is remarkable. This beautiful country is a melting pot of many different cultures. Its history stretches from Roman times, to the reign of Bosnian kings, from the Ottoman period which ruled for four centuries to another four centuries of Austro-Hungarian rule and the Yugoslavian era with Marshal Tito as its leader.

The countryside is a paradise for nature lovers, rugged mountains beckon skiers, rivers invite rafting, kayaking or canoeing. And let's not forget the delicious food and hospitality of the people.

Do try cevapi (grilled minced meat fingers) but if your appetite is slim don't do as I did and ask on arrival in Sarevejo's old Turkish quarter, Bascarsija, for a chicken sandwich. Just a small one, I said. What arrived was a huge Turkish-like pizza filled with chicken and heaps of salad. I ate one quarter of it. I heard one visitor remark that this area of rambling cobblestone streets straddling the mosques and minarets was more oriental than Istanbul. The bazaars showcase Bosnians' talents as gold, silver and coppersmiths,. Here you will find their creative legacy to the war – shell casings and bullets fashioned into ballpoint pens.

I stayed in private accommodation organised by the Halvat guest house in the old town, for forty kmarks (about $34) a night. It was the owner's late grandfather's house – the guest house was full. I had two rooms and a bathroom, plus a garden and view of the spring-blossomed hills. A hot breakfast down a steep hill to the guest house was about the equivalent of $6, but numerous coffee houses abound, offering very cheap food. At night I wandered down a side street and found the bar Zlatna Ribica on Kapitol 5. It's ideal for an evening beer or cocktail or, for something even livelier, the City Pub was a must for its live music and raucous atmosphere.

On a walking tour, the young guide told me she was ten during the war which destroyed so much of her city but she still went to school every day. There are still signs of the war like the market place branded with the names of the civilians killed there during bombings, but people have gone back to living their lives as before, side by side with many denominations and cultures.

I reflected too on another war which changed history: near the Latin Bridge, the heir to the Austro-Hungarian throne, Franz Ferdinand,

and his pregnant wife Sophia were assassinated, an event that triggered World War I.

Next visit I will go to the old town of Mostar, proclaimed a UNESCO World Heritage site, and to the nearby art colony of Pocitelj.

Dressed for a Vienna ball.

Fortune telling at an international summer school fete in England.

Villagers prepare bread for baking at the Transylvania village of Palatka.

The old town of Budva, Montenegro.

The market area of Sarajevo.

The Kolar family at their Tunnel Museum, Sarajevo.

The island of Korcula, Croatia.

Budapest, winter 2009. (Photo: Nicola Brackett)

14
Recession stalled among wild beauty, 2008

Winter in Europe. But here was warm sun, shaded by the ancient walls of a 2,000-year-old tower. The only sign of winter was the cold lap of the Adriatic against my bare feet.

After four years living in Budapest and falling for Croatia on my first visit there, I moved to the latter's cheaper neighbour, Montenegro, in January 2008, and soon discovered it was experiencing one of the biggest tourism booms in the region.

Settled into a small studio apartment with a view of sea and mountains in the country's most popular summer resort, Budva, ceaseless hammering and drilling relentlessly reminded me of this boom. And despite the worldwide recession it still expected 2.5 per cent economic growth in 2009 and beyond, based on planned foreign direct investment into new developments as well as projects that had already begun. This according to an interview I had with Nada Medenica, the country's Deputy Minister for Economic Development.

One site was destined to become a mega mall full of shops, a cinema and leisure centre. Locals were resigned to the noise – permission had been given, they told me, for the work to continue all hours till the first tourist load arrived around early May. After all, they shrugged, tourism is our main industry.

Budva might be one big construction site in the new part of the town, at least, but it didn't detract from the glorious views across the bays and old town thrusting into the Adriatic. In the summer it becomes a big open-air theatre of local and international performances. Madonna visited in 2008, and the Rolling Stones the year before. Go in off season, or at least April – winters do get cold, even though I had a paddle on 26 January – and miss the masses of July and August.

Montenegro is wilder and more rugged than Croatia, hence its description 'wild beauty' in the tourist brochures. A small country of around 14,000 square kilometres, its scenery is spectacular and varied. Once outside the medieval towns of the coast like Budva, Bar, Ulcinj and Kotor, soaring, snow-capped mountains, deep river gorges and the Tara canyon were impressive but getting there by car proved a nightmare along the narrow twisting road, the main highway to Belgrade, where cars and trucks overtake blithely on blind corners. The road is often blocked in the winter. Podgorica, the capital, had little of particular interest despite having the most expensive hotels in the country. Much more picturesque was the former capital, Cetinje, a charming town full of the history of this small, proud and friendly nation.

The seventy-three kilometres of coastline to Ulcinj and the Albanian border include gems like Kotor, with its ancient old town, dating back to the twelfth and fourteenth centuries. A 4.5-kilometre-long town wall from the Byzantine period was fortified by the Venetians and Austrians.

Kotor is said to have about seventy per cent of the cultural and historical monuments of Montenegro. Add to this Boka Kotorska Bay, a majestic fjord about 105 kilometres long, of which twenty-five kilometres is in Kotor Bay, and you can understand why Kotor is being dubbed the Monte Carlo of Eastern Europe, although in my view there is no comparison – magnificent Kotor stands alone. Stroll around the village of Prcanj, eight kilometres from Kotor, and you would think you were in Italy, or Provence even, lovely old stone houses line the waterfront, where boats bob lazily and the locals chat at quaint cafés facing the fjord.

South to the modern port of Bar and it was hard to believe that this is an ancient town. My two American teacher colleagues and I took a six-kilometre taxi ride to the old town – the place was mentioned in ninth century papers under the name Anivari. This Montenegrin Pompeii houses the ruins of around 240 houses, churches and palaces. On that day, storm clouds over the high peaks created a ghostly atmosphere on the Londza Plateau where the town stands.

The Montenegrins captured it from the Turks in 1878. During

massive shellings, most of the buildings were ruined, lightning struck an ammunitions warehouse in 1881, and a similar explosion in 1912 destroyed much more. But the ruined fortress has found new life as an open-air theatre in summer. On the way back from the steep climb, we slid off the slippery cobbled street to a delicious fish soup at the Spilja Restaurant, the building's bizarrely twisted wooden facade reminiscent of a Swiss chalet the Swiss would have soundly rejected.

In Ulcinj, the Orient meets the Occident. Mosques and minarets are common, legacy of the conquering Turks. A stopover before the one-hour bus ride the next day into Albania cost us three travellers seven euros each for a room. In the old town – another more than two and half millennia old – we stayed in a private house run by very hospitable Albanians. The weather was shocking, crashing waves and pouring rain, very cold, no heating in the rooms. 'It doesn't get cold,' said the host. Montenegro doesn't go in for ducted heating or much heating at all in winter. Maybe it's something to do with its rugged mountain man image.

Cruising took on a new twist that evening as we fought against the wind to get to a café on the waterfront, in vain seeking a non-smoking area in this full-on smoking country where everyone seems to ignore the law not to smoke in public areas. We watched intrigued as tight groups of young men wandered slowly to a pole or small barrier beside the water, did an about turn and walked back a few metres to another post and so on and so forth, with no set purpose, it seemed, but to talk incessantly in this language that is phonetic, so easy to pronounce if not to learn.

Ulcinj has probably one of the most fascinating histories in Montenegro. The Turks lost the sea battle of Lepanto in 1571 and offered Unicinj, as it was then called, as a home for 400 surviving pirates who had fought with the Turks. But instead of quietly stashing away their cutlasses, they became so powerful that no town or ship on the Adriatic was secure. Ulcinj became the trading post for the plundered goods and a major slave market evolved. Some say the Turks finally burned the ships of the bandits.

If you get this far, you may as well take the bus into Albania and the first town of Skhodra; the capital Tirana is about another three hours away. The most startling images were the small concrete bunkers in every garden on the way, disfiguring so much of the Albanian landscape. The former dictator, Enver Hoxha, put up 600,000 of them. This was ostensibly to repel attack from whatever quarter it might come, but in reality created a surreal atmosphere of permanent insecurity amongst the population. Skhodra itself is full of buildings painted in bright gelato colours, very friendly people and cheap, tasty food. A cardboard kangaroo clutching a Fosters beer graced the front of one popular café.

I can't leave the Montenegro coast without having mentioned Sveti Stefan, the private island and hotel, now under renovation, frequented by the rich and famous. Once a fisherman's village, it has been a holiday haven for stars such as Sophia Loren, Sylvester Stallone, Kirk Douglas, Elizabeth Taylor and the late Princess Margaret of England.

The inland delights of this compact country need to be thoroughly savoured as well. What the Alps are for the Swiss, the Durmitors are for the Montenegrins. Durmitor National Park in the north-east of the country has many different landscapes in its 32,000 hectares. Canyons, mountains, plateaus, with a Mediterranean as well as alpine climate. Rushing rivers great for white-water rafting, bears wandering the mountains and the wonders of the vast Skadar lake, which also straddles Albania. There is a major bird sanctuary as well as the biggest natural fresh water reservoir. There are fifty islands in the lake, some with ruins of churches and monasteries.

Montenegro's most famous monastery is Ostrog, one of the most important centres of the Serbian Orthodox Church. Built into the rocks, it is 900 metres above the Zeta valley. You turn off the main road between Podgorica and the town of Niksic. It was a highlight of my time there, despite the frightening but thankfully short ride along hairpin bends by a hired driver – the cars wait to pick up passengers off the bus from Podgorica. He kept turning around to me hanging grimly to the back seat, once asking smugly if I was scared. I said nothing, just smiled between gritted teeth and tried not to look down as we barely missed falling off a cliff.

Finally, a point about the culture. If Montenegrins invite you out, don't offer to pay anything or go dutch, they will be very offended. Simply expect to pay next time. You will definitely need a phrase book; English is sparse, even in some of the larger hotels.

15
The sworn virgins of Montenegro & Albania

I met academic Aleksandra Djajic Horvath in Florence because I wanted to write about her doctoral thesis on the 'sworn virgins' of Montenegro and Albania and maybe find some of them. It was a story that had fascinated me for some time since hearing it from a close friend of Aleksandra's in Budapest.

A girl could declare she had become a male and was brought up dressed as a boy/man, carrying a weapon and upholding the family honour in blood feuds. The sworn virgin swears to celibacy for life, The 200-year-old custom derives not from religious beliefs but from traditional law. Women belonged to their fathers until marriage, when they became their husband's property. Some women chose the male life, to escape arranged, unwanted marriages without dishonouring the would-be groom and his family. The phenomenon does not undermine the patriarchy; rather it allows women, often confined to a subordinate role, a freer way of life. Most of the women are now in their sixties and older.

Aleksandra wrote her thesis (titled 'Tobelija or woman in man's costume – socially approved female transvestism in the patriarchal Balkans in the 19th and 20th centuries') on these women while a PhD researcher at the Department of History and Civilization, European University Institute, Florence, Italy.

In a paper published in the *Anthropology Matters* journal 2002–3, she describes how at the beginning of the second half of the nineteenth century an intriguing phenomenon was registered in the Dinaric mountain belt in the western Balkan peninsula. In 1855, while carrying out fieldwork among the Rovci tribe on the border of Herzegovina and Montenegro, Milorad Medakovic, a Serbian ethnographer, came across a case of a girl called Milica who, not having any brothers, vowed to stay unmarried in order to be a surrogate son to her father. The girl wore male clothes and arms, and was accorded the same respect in her community as a man.

Almost at the same time, Johann Georg von Hahn, an Austrian consul in the Balkans and a distinguished Albanologist, discovered a couple of similar cases of *tobelija* among the tribes of northern Albania, which he described in his book *Reise durch die Gebiete des Drin und Wardar*. Published in Vienna in 1867, his book recounts a meeting with four Albanian girls who publicly renounced marriage and decided to change their gender. Hahn describes two of the girls' motives for making such a change, reporting that one decided on this course of action because she had been in love with a man who she could not marry, while the other had not wanted to marry a man her parents had chosen because he was not of the same religion.

This female-to-male transformation, conditional on a denial of sexuality and absolute celibacy, resulted not only in the acquisition of a male name, male clothes and a male haircut, but also of certain male privileges, such as possessing and carrying arms, socialising freely with men, and participating in men's assemblies.

Aleksandra, from the former Yugolavia, and her husband met one of these men/women in the mountains of Montenegro. Seated in her office at the university in Florence, with views through the windows to the Tuscan hills, it was easy to imagine, as Aleksandra told it, those wilder hills and mountains where the elderly woman insisted on speaking directly to the academic's husband – assuming he was the researcher. Aleksandra did not enlighten her, as this seemed to be the easier solution to securing an interview. It was not only a difficult journey but proved almost impossible to locate her. She was found working alone tending animals in the high pastures, living in a small cabin and seemingly contented with the life she had chosen.

Aleksandra advised me not to go alone if I decided to search for them, as the terrain was not only rugged and often treacherous in unpredictable weather but I would probably encounter hostility without a male companion. Reluctantly I abandoned the idea. The trek did not deter British researcher, Antonia Young, who has also published material on these women. In an article in *The Guardian* of 31 March 2007, she describes how one, now seventy-seven, became the 'man' of the house when she was twelve after her father was killed by Serb forces because he was with the resistance. She said she had once wanted to be a man, would like to marry now, but it was too late. Another, of forty-nine, was given male status by her father when she was five, because he decided he wanted another son (there was an older brother). She now wishes she could have children of her own but is resigned to the fact she cannot be a woman now.

16
Krakow, the salt mines and Auschwitz

An overnight train from Budapest to medieval Krakow, once the capital of Poland, and the following day a thirty-minute bus ride took me and a friend to the UNESCO World Heritage Wieliczka Salt Mine, often referred to as 'the Underground Salt Cathedral of Poland'.

Tourist agencies report that over a million tourists visit it yearly, and they seemed to be all there on this national holiday. You can see artistic carvings, lovingly fashioned by the miners. Chandeliers, chapels, the seven dwarfs and Snow White...salt everywhere. We kept turning around to admire, often, like Lot's wife, frozen in our tracks. A visit to the mine is also supposed to be beneficial for upper respiratory illnesses or allergies, treatment taking place in a special chamber.

The older works were sculpted by miners out of rock salt and there are more recent figures by contemporary artists. Even the crystals of the chandeliers are made from rock salt that was dissolved and reconstituted to achieve a clear, glass-like appearance. Also featured is a large chamber with walls carved to resemble wooden chapels built by miners in earlier centuries; an underground lake; and exhibits on the history of salt mining. Get a personal guide if you can. We paid a bit extra for one to avoid the queues, it was well worth it.

Auschwitz-Birkenau is about an hour from Krakow. So much has been written about these death camps that I will not dwell on my visit. Suffice to say that it was impossible to comprehend so much horror inflicted by human beings on their own. Surreal too because of the conveyor belt aspect of the visit – robot-like tourists going in, coming out, the guide reciting monologue-fashion inconceivable numbers of deaths and facts. I asked her afterwards how she could speak so dispassionately. She replied that she had grown up in the area, the horrendous events were so much a part of her life and, anyway, she could not afford to be emotional in her job.

17
Berlin and the Ampelmannchen

When the Berlin wall collapsed in 1989, I had just begun a diplomatic posting in Brussels. A group of us dashed off one long weekend to collect souvenirs of the wall. As we drove into the east, joining the streams of cars heading that way, chugging out towards us were hundreds of noisy, polluting, two-stroke Trabant cars. We watched them break down and their frustrated drivers and crammed in passengers spill out from the can-like interiors, as the Mercedes and BMWs whizzed past. I will always remember this auto symbol of liberation.

The bits of the wall I collected were thrown out later by a housekeeper who thought the pieces lined up on my mantelpiece were dirt but, fourteen years later, returning to Berlin for a conference, I only found large chunks as replacements. A thin line on the road indicated where the original wall had stood. The open wasteland beyond it of 1989 was now the Potsdam Plaza. Searching for a cinema there, I got lost in its maze like depths.

However, I did bring back one unusual souvenir of unification which prompts much curiosity when I wear it. It is a reminder of one of the first disagreements between the once divided city – a sweatshirt emblazoned with the former GDR traffic signs. After German re-unification in 1990, there were attempts to standardise all traffic signs to the West German forms. East German street signs and traffic signs were dismantled and replaced because of differing fonts in the former two German countries. But the East Berliners wanted the *Ampelmannchen* (little traffic light man) back, started campaigning and won. Now you can buy the red and green traffic symbol as a souvenir.

18
The Czech Republic

I first visited Prague a year after the Velvet Revolution in 1989. My husband and I stayed in an apartment we had rented from some Belgium friends in the suburbs, about twenty-five minutes on the Metro – then quite dilapidated, but efficient nevertheless. The city was overrun by expensively furred Italians and young entrepreneurial types, mostly Americans, if you could believe the Czech people's grumblings about a US invasion. Our apartment was adequate but gloomy in a grey concrete block, the residents queueing nearby for suspect fruit and cheap vegetables.

When I returned in 2005, Prague had enthusiastically embraced tourism, or perhaps it was the other way round. Mindful of the boost to its economy, attractions abounded, tour guides leading a glut of nationalities through its ancient sights. The Metro was suitably upgraded and there was a general air of prosperity but I soon decided other European cities had more attractions to offer than Prague. I also compared it with one about three hours' bus ride away – Cesky Krumlow. This is a unique historical town, also UNESCO-listed, smaller than Prague but much cheaper and without the tourist crush. It had a toy town feel about it, frozen in time, very hospitable and worth a two-day stay.

19
Slovakia

Ever since the Slavs were invaded by the Magyars (Hungarians), over 1,000 years ago, there has been some tension between the two countries over certain issues. The two-hour train ride from Budapest to the capital, Bratislava, was uneventful, apart from a carriage companion, an American teacher, who regaled me with tales of her days of hiking in the spectacular peaks of the high Tatra mountains of Slovakia. The only hiking I was going to do was probably two hours with the Vienna and Bratislava Hash House Harriers.

We bypassed the old town, instead jogging beside canals and through woods and stopping for beer, as is the tradition of this group. Both stops were memorable. The first, buried in a forest, was a tavern playing very loud American country and western music and proudly displaying the Stars and Stripes. Why? Seemed there was no American connection with the place. The other was a steakhouse closer to the city, an array of motorcycles parked outside, including some pretty swish Harleys. It was a loud, fun place, becoming even more interesting after each drink, and promising 'boy and girl strippers' at 11 p.m. Unfortunately I had to catch a 10.30 p.m. train back.

The second visit in 2007 was a sudden decision, a late evening car dash from Budapest to a party in Bratislava. Arriving at 11 p.m., we mixed with mostly Germans who had set up businesses in Slovakia because of the uniform tax rate of nineteen per cent on citizens (and often companies) regardless of income (it's changed a bit now). The party was also getting interesting but we had to leave to make the round trip within twelve hours as one of our group thought her visa would expire after that. She was mistaken, we could have stayed, but at least we had time to check out the old town, small but jumping, before speeding off.

More time was given to Croatia – the most beautiful country I have seen.

20
Croatia

Setting off for two weeks' driving in Croatia with a friend I remembered a man surprising me at a Sydney party by describing Croatia as the most beautiful country in the world. I guess I had associated it too much with war and not its previous life as a popular tourist destination when part of the former Yugoslavia. Now, after several visits, I agree with him.

Spectacular islands, with ancient towns encased by city walls (Korcula, supposedly the birthplace of Marco Polo, is a mini Dubrovnik). National parks, stunning coastline, friendly people, great food and wonderful music. The only things missing are plenty of sandy beaches but the Adriatic is so wonderfully clear it's not so important.

I sought out the tiny island of Susak to find out about the little-known language spoken there, and found a story of an immigration of many of its people to New Jersey, taking the archaic dialect – a mix of old Croatian, English, Italian and French – with them. I was lucky enough to meet some of the second generation holidaying on Susak with their immigrant parents – successful young Americans, some of whom ironically wanted to leave their highly paid jobs and return to their parents' former homeland to live. In fact, more than eighty per cent of Susak's population left at the end of World War II and in the mid-1960s, escaping, like one man, now in his sixties, told me, from Marshal Tito's regime, by boat via Italy and to Hoboken, New Jersey. They didn't want to stay under the Tito plan because there were few rewards for work. 'The US offered more, and I had relatives who had gone to New Jersey before the war and found work in the shipbuilding industry there,' he said.

Many villagers wear the folk costumes unique to the island. Known as the sandy island, it is connected by ferry to the island of Losinj and the town of Rijeka, both well worth a visit, Losinj with its Venetian ambience like so many of the islands on this part of the coast.

Croatia's neighbour, Slovenia, is another former, enticing slice of the Austro-Hungarian empire.

21
Slovenia

My son Shaun, visiting from Australia, and I stayed in a delightful, cheap pension surrounded by the majestic Julian Alps. At renowned Lake Bled, with its island, thermal springs and medieval castle, we admired magnificent views. Later, dodging the other tourists, we went to the charming capital, Ljubljana, where we tracked down a young Slovenian woman we had met in Hungary who was working for one of the larger recruiting agencies in the city. A wise move, as she introduced us to some very tasty traditional Slovenian food, urging us to try goulash. 'But that's Hungarian,' we protested. This dish, however, was much richer and meatier with thick chunks of beef, lashings of mushrooms, spices, and a dash of something alcoholic I couldn't pick. All cooked in a pot at your table.

Ljubljana's baroque old town, nestling at the foot of Castle Hill, is claimed to have been founded by the mythical Greek prince, Jason. While fleeing with the stolen Golden Fleece, Jason and his companions, the Argonauts sailed from the Black Sea up the Danube, from the Danube into the Sava, and from the Sava into the Ljubljanica. Here he slew the so called Ljubljana dragon. The dragon is now on the Ljubljana coat of arms on the top of the castle tower.

A later visit found me and a companion at Lake Bohinj, set in wilder scenery than around Bled, an hour north. We stayed in rooms (about $15 a night) in a private house in a small village. From the window we could see a chuckling stream, mountains, a friendly tavern and a few hikers. We walked around the large lake, into the hills, and then – he – into the mountains, with a sweater and a lot of stamina, returning tired, dirty and hungry just as I was about to summon a rescue party.

19
How's your love life?

'Any romances? How's your love life?' I am asked these questions frequently

In Chuuk, the women all fell for the tall, athletic American Peace Corps volunteer with the ponytail, and his way of making a woman feel she was the only one on earth. Eyes locked, laughing at her feeble jokes (mine were feeble anyway). I invited him for a meal in my hotel room. I sat close while he ignored me and reminisced about the lost love of his life and how he hadn't really recovered. A not so subtle back-off hint for me. Next I saw a new volunteer getting the intensive eye lock treatment and rapidly recovered.

There was my Budapest man, who lasted on and off for nearly three years. Not Hungarian, but New Zealand born, a traveller like myself, restless but caught no doubt between the strange guilt, or is it fear, of thinking you should stay put and the urge for moving on. We moved on. In opposite directions. But by joining in Hungary's in-your-face daily love-in (although not so blatantly), I stopped being jealous for a while.

A Montenegrin woman friend told me that the Montenegrin men control their women and the Serbian men do the housework. So I made friends with a Serbian-Australian man, who was bringing up his ten-year-old twins alone after his wife left him. He was an oddity in this traditional society of specific roles for men and women, so he did not seem to have many male friends. He was constantly asking me about my past relationships as if I was an expert on sustaining good ones.

After harbouring early lustful ideas, I also bounced back quite quickly after disagreements on basic issues like 'Why don't you get a babysitter and come out for the night?'

'Because my responsibility is to my children.'

'But you keep going on about wanting to meet someone.'

'Yes, but she has to understand my kids come first.'

He called sometimes very late to meet at a bar when I was either in bed or about to go. Any life in a summer resort in winter was beguiling, however late.

Germany, briefly. I worked there for four months. There was an intriguing man. A communist intellectual (his words) and radical. We recited poetry to each other or told jokes all night, or danced affectionately for hours at his home, before he took me to my train home and spent the night with his estranged wife. I was amazed at my tolerance then but the real cut came when he announced he preferred flat-chested women who needed rescuing – definitely not me.

From this you will gather that romance in the true sense has eluded me in my travels. No sweeping off the feet, with longer-term happiness beckoning, or an outcome of long-lasting friendship despite the end of whatever it was or might have been.

An adventure still to come.

20
A different relationship, Budapest 2009

In an unexpected return of six months to Budapest, I wonder again what keeps drawing me back. The city is such a contrast. Often shabby. Often beautiful. I have lived in three different apartments in the thirteenth district of Pest; it's my patch now. A short walk to the Danube – that amazing river which from source to delta runs a whole 2,840 kilometres, passing through eight different countries before spilling into the Black Sea.

I once walked through Nyugati metro station, where homeless people curl up together for warmth, and, nearing a rubbish bin, stopped short at the incongruous sight of two legs protruding from its depths, a loud snore shaking the receptacle's sides. My boyfriend of that time took one scathing look and pronounced he'd had it with Budapest and would leave. So he did. But I continue to metaphorically search for the flowers among the weeds and usually found them peeking out unexpectedly in this unpredictable city.

As I headed off around 6.30 a.m. most mornings to teach students before they worked, I had to look down for the dog droppings and late-night vomit. I was muttering one morning about lack of government initiative to lead and encourage people to care about their environment more when I noticed something different in some of the dingier streets near my home – flowers. Nothing metaphorical about these pretty baskets colourfully hanging in lines.

Glimpses of the old face of socialism glared down from paint-cracked buildings. But when I looked higher, the blocks of buildings and districts were not always uniform in style, giving Budapest its unique eclectic architecture. The Classicist, Romanesque, Gothic and Art Nouveau architecture was predominantly shaped by the master architects of the nineteenth century. Buildings built during Roman times and the Turkish occupation of the country still can be found.

The mix was often startling, especially for those who venture off a main street through an open gateway into a hidden courtyard. Like when I left a busy main road on a balmy day, wandered through an open gate and found myself in a spacious, cobbled courtyard, redolent with magnolia from a nearby park and gracious buildings, clustered around the Sandor Petofi museum named after Hungary's most famous poet, who in 1848 inspired a revolution for independence from Austrian Habsburg rule but died a year later in another battle near Segesvar against the Russians. He was twenty-six. It's believed that he is buried in a mass grave along with other Hungarian soldiers who died in the battle.

Petőfi was co-author and, respectively, author of what are considered as two of Hungary's most important written documents: the *12 Pont* (demands to the Habsburg Governor-General) and the *Nemezeti Dal*: *National Song*. Unfortunately some important museums, like the Petofi one, have only information in Hungarian, which deters tourists from visiting. A shortcoming for a city that wants tourists.

When did it feel like home? More so then, surprising me, as I hadn't intended living there again. But also when I first returned in 2007 and coming from the airport saw the magnificently coloured Zsolnay-tiled roof of the Museum of Applied Arts (pyrogranite is a form of ornamental ceramics which Zsolnay Vilmos developed in 1886, followed seven years later by the eosin glazing process which gives the famous Zsolnay porcelain an iridescent lustre). The tiles adorn many roofs throughout Budapest and other parts of Hungary, particularly the southern town of Pecs where Zsolnay was born.

When I stopped in the centre of the chain bridge one soft summer night, after visiting friends in Buda, I looked across the Danube at the lights of Buda and of Pest and the great illuminated towers of parliament house. And there it was. A deep warmth for a place I had no connection with traditionally or historically or through family. Although my longer-term future plans are uncertain as I prepare to return to Australia for a period, I know I can always come back.

So have I simply moved geographically, or is there a more profound change? The answer to the latter cannot be a simple yes when circumstance can change your life without choice. When I returned to Australia in 2006, I was recovering from a broken relationship and the end of a job, again. It was almost a repeat of 1996, although not so devastating as when I returned to the loss of a diplomatic career and the rawness of grief when the shock dissipates after sudden death. Thus my return on those two occasions was tainted by bereavement. I adjusted slowly, gained a teaching certificate and left again.

Returning to Budapest in 2007 was difficult emotionally because of the end of that relationship, mainly conducted in that city, finishing acrimoniously and biting harder than I expected, as familiar places didn't yield that familiar face. I left in 2008 because I was offered what appeared to be more secure contracts in Montenegro and Germany.

Six months in Budapest in 2009 was different. I related to the city in a way I had not done before. It wasn't the people, the traditions, not even the friends, who were very important after a barren stretch in Germany when my job as a teacher with a US company ended abruptly after training programs were axed, but simply the place. I had been asked in Germany if I was searching for something. 'Yes,' I replied. 'Home.' Without hesitation. Then wondered what I meant by that.

I believe I have been happier overseas because of the many challenges. I have adapted to new cultures, languages, become more self-sufficient and learned not to be afraid of being on my own – I once sought constant diversion to stave off potential loneliness and keep sadness at bay. That is not to say that it doesn't get lonely after a while for lack of someone to talk to in your own language or lack of company, of course it does, but I have learned to deal with that and use my resources more efficiently. All this should result in a more positive shift in my previous character, I believe. The real beginnings, I hope, of forging a more compelling mark on my life.

Budapest and the Central and Eastern European region feels like home because we connect. But it is one of my homes not *the* one. I am hoping to have the same feeling again for Australia. That depth of feeling I once had for landscape. For the rich ochres and reds and desert yellows. And the great sense of distance that is so different from Europe. I once thought special people made a place home and it is still true but I also now believe that a place can have the same effect – even on your first visit.

21
Sydney, January 2010

I have been back for six months. It has not been an easy adjustment. In the past seven years of travelling I have not felt such a distinctive sense of the negatives of sudden change and its incumbent almost grief-like emotions as I have felt on my returns to Australia since 1996. The place is not home any more. The sense of home is in the company of family and friends. For now I feel exposed and rather raw. This country is heavy with memory, like England where I grew up.

I acknowledge that my feelings for the Australia I grew to love from my arrival as a migrant of twenty markedly changed in 1995 and 1996 when my life as I had known it died with my husband and the loss of my career overseas and with it a promised post in Bonn which would have given me a new direction. Add to this the obvious fact that living in other countries for long periods blurs the edges of what constitutes home and, in my case, prompted a re-evaluation of where I felt most comfortable and stimulated – then I begin to understand where that sense of belonging I seek may be.

I grew up and was educated in England but have no interest in living there again. However, I have retained strong links with school friends. When I immigrated to Australia with my husband Ron, the call of the exotic outweighed what was being left behind. To me, it was a rather dismal English town which bored me. My mother actually came with us then, so leaving family was not an issue, although she did return to stay in England and remarried.

What I did not realise then was that I was leaving behind what has now become integral to my search for identity and a sense of belonging: my European roots. In 1966 when I walked onto the Italian migrant ship *Castele Felice* in Southampton, England, joining the hundreds of others seeking a so-called better life five weeks and 12,000 miles away, I had no concept that I was giving up a continent of which I was a part. For what? Why didn't I stay and live on that continent with its many cultures and languages, its variety and vitality? Why didn't I stay and learn other languages so I could work there and experience all that it had to offer? So England didn't appeal but it was a stepping stone to so much across that short stretch of channel. Those questions were only asked twenty-three years later when I worked in Brussels, and Europe was so much more attractive than forty years before. Many of those early migrants, or at least their offspring, have returned. I recall talking to a distressed Greek-Australian father in Sydney some years ago on just that ironic point. His Australian-born son was living in Greece with his Greek girlfriend. His daughter was also living in Europe. He was one of those parents who sought better lives for their families in far places only to see them return to the ancestral lands.

I had been friends with the late Australian writer Randolph Stow since discovering in 1993 he was living in my former home town of Harwich, Essex, in England and I published articles, with his permission, about our first meeting. He too returned to his ancestral roots of Suffolk and Essex about the same time as I went to Australia and felt connected with this region of England although he was born in Western Australia. He considered himself Anglo-Australian and few people in Harwich, where his nickname was Mick, knew he was a writer. He was occasionally mistaken for a seaman or truck driver, or worker at the local factory as he wandered in its direction with a canvas bag. In winter he looked more like a sailor in thick jeans and sweater, drawn to the unknown quality of the sea he loved. He felt he lived among people touched by that unpredictability. He showed me new and enlightening aspects of the rather depressing town I left, especially its history as the start of a Pilgrim Fathers' voyage to America in the *Mayflower*. The ship's captain was a Harwich man, Christopher Jones, his house is not far from where I was born. Samuel Pepys was once a Harwich MP and Admiral Lord Nelson was stationed there.

Since Stow's death in May 2010, which was a great shock as we did not email – he rejected it – I have recalled our conversations. I would call him when in England to visit my now late mother. We would stroll to a local pub or restaurant from his home with its door adorned with a mask of that pagan heralder of spring, the Green Man. I am still puzzled why his birthplace was not important to him. Although I have no interest in living in England I have embraced the diversity of the European continent like a long-lost deserter.

When I published the first article about meeting him in Harwich, I said he had led me to examine my rejection of my home town and native land with curiosity and a growing recognition that I had not been entirely fair to my heritage. He was very much a part of the community of Harwich, and as an explorer of the effects of exile and alienation which dominated his later work, he seemed to have finally found a painless exile, unlike the migrant – once described to me as the world's greatest spectator – who can often be pulled between two lands, the native one and the chosen one. The roots can become painfully twisted, creating a continual restless search.

Yet in 1966 (and for many years) Australia caught me and wove its magic. Made me try and keep trying harder to adapt and adjust. To forge a successful career, sustain a long marriage, have a son, make lifelong friends and miss it terribly many times, particularly on first working stints overseas before 1995. Now Europe appears to have me under its spell as never before. Does that mean my time is done in Australia? Not while I have family and friends here. But something seems to have ended and something different a world away has struck a deep and unexpected chord.

In my introduction I referred to Jung's theory of individuation, which I interpreted simply as the need to create something different from who we have been. Travelling and taking on work I had never done before, meeting challenges alone and surmounting them has led to greater self-reliance but not to any profound fundamental change in my character. Any indelible mark I strive to leave has yet to be carved. When a trigger stirs loss and pain, I go through it, accept that it will pass and try to remain as cheerful and grateful as possible for the opportunities for constant discovery about place and self.

22
Sydney, March 2011

I returned to England in December 2010 for a memorial service for my mother, who had died suddenly in May of that year. While acknowledging that one of the main reasons I had lived in Europe was gone, I was sure my earlier feelings for Budapest would be intact when I arrived in the city some weeks later for a short visit.

It may have been my bereavement and the lack of support from friends scattered elsewhere for the holidays but, inexplicably, there was not the same sense of home as before.

Australia is also not 'home' but in this interim period when I struggle with what strangely feels like homesickness for a strong sense of home that now eludes me, and grieve for the loss of my only parent, something fresh for me, rich with ideas, is emerging – despite resistance – in this adopted country of mine.

I will finish this book as I began it, with a Jungian view which has influenced my journeying.

What prevents people from becoming autonomous, fulfilled and ultimately happy is their refusal to open themselves to experiences that are new and unfamiliar, and thus potentially threatening to their sense of self.

'Something in us wishes to remain a child, to be unconscious or, at most, conscious only of the ego; to reject everything strange, or else subject it to our will; to do nothing, or else indulge our own craving for pleasure or power.' – Carl Jung, *The Structures and Dynamics of the Psyche*

A view from Buda across the Danube to downtown Pest.

www.ingramcontent.com/pod-product-compliance
Lightning Source LLC
Chambersburg PA
CBHW062152100526
44589CB00014B/1806